The Wall

PITT POETRY SERIES
Ed Ochester, Editor

THE
WALL

ILAN
STAVANS

University of Pittsburgh Press

Published by the University of Pittsburgh Press, Pittsburgh, Pa., 15260
Copyright © 2018, Ilan Stavans
All rights reserved
Manufactured in the United States of America
Printed on acid-free paper
10 9 8 7 6 5 4 3 2 1

ISBN 13: 978-0-8229-6528-2
ISBN 10: 0-8229-6528-3

Cover photograph © Alex Webb / Magnum Photos
Cover design by Alex Wolfe

For Edwin Cruz,
soñador

We are all lumps, and of so various and inform a contexture, that every piece plays, every moment, its own game, and there is as much difference betwixt us and ourselves as betwixt us and others.

—MICHEL DE MONTAIGNE,
"Of the Inconstancy of Our Actions"

CONTENTS

I. THE EDGE OF THE KINGDOM

Doleful,
       confine—
incision
of despair:
    margin,
    precipice,
    limbo,
    you
    slash
the body
into
    bulges
    and
        puncture
        the
        soul.

Shipwrecked
in
a disconsolate
    country,
        in
        a
    century
built
through
resentment,
for
six
days

(y
sus
noches),
I,
alone,
unencumbered,
traverse
the
land,
like
Álvar Núñez Cabeza de Vaca,
in
search
of
ghosts:
the
mother
whose
love
for
her
son
has
soured,
the
adopted
child
in
search
of
genesis,
the
brother
with
a
heart

condition
looking
    for
        a
            doctor
        to
    cure
him.
I
am
an abstraction:
my
imagination,
free,
scans
the emotional
landscape.
Places
are
sites
where
fantasy
meets
recognition.
           Reality
           is
           such
           an
           aberration,
           it
           is okay
           to
           go
           crazy.
Nihil
humanum

a
me
alienum
puto.
But
humans
are
aliens
to themselves.
The
happy
socialize
with
the
happy,
the
powerful
with
the
powerful.
And,
far behind,
in
a
ghetto,
is
poverty
and
misfortune.
I
survey
in
order
to
build
a

cartography
of
what
was
and
will
be.
Today
           gives
                   place
                           to the past
                   as
           the future
is
           born.
                           Maps,
                                   Joseph Conrad
                           said,
                           were
                           "blank spaces"
                           that
                           became
                           "places
                           of
                           darkness."
Maps
are
traps.
The
true
world
is
outside,
beyond,
uncontained.
Yo

soy
el
mapa
de
mí
mismo.

A
tumultuous wall
keeps
them
asunder.

      I
start
at
the start:
in the unbridled
            clash
        of
            rivalries—
        howls
        and
            roars
            and
            whines
            and
            hollers—,
        I
come across,
            on
            the
            beach
            in
            Bagdad,
                Tamaulipas,

where
caravans
of
camels
carried
salt
during
the American Civil War,
a
town
that
ceased
to exist
in
1880.
The
floodplains
remain
but
not the dreams.
Yo
solo,
sin
alma,
surrounded
by
unexpected
calm.
Where
is
the
fury
I
see
on
TV?

Where
are
the
ill-disposed
    neighbors?

It
all
starts
for
me
in
a
never-ending
room,
its
boundaries
as
far
as the eye
can
see.
This
is
our playground:
day in
and
day out,
my
brother
and
I,
ages
5
and
7,

　　　　run
　　　　　　around,
back
　　　　and forth,
once
upon
a noontime dreary,
　　　　　　　incessantly,
　　　　without
stop,
　　　　until
we
are comfortably
numb.
Three
cold,
white
　　　　walls,
　　　　on
　　　　which
　　　　we
　　　　are
　　　　invited
　　　　to
　　　　draw
　　　　with
　　　　crayons,
　　　　markers,
　　　　paint brushes.
　　　　The
　　　　wooden
　　　　floor
　　　　is
　　　　ideal
　　　　for
　　　　sledding.

The
fourth
wall
is
made
of
windows:

we
are
inside
a
fish-bowl.

Bikes,
fútbol,
grand
guignol.
Joy
is
ignorance;
ignorance
is
bliss.

But
to
moody
teenagers
a
few
years
later,
the
same room
looks
small,

                                        compressed,
                                        unprivate.
Mine
            is
                                        mine,
                                        not
            yours.
Rough
are
the
            rival
            sides
                            of
            sibling
            love.
            Family
            relations
            are
            a
            web
            of
            conflicted
            loyalties.
            Ask
                            Regan,
                            Goneril,
                            and
                            Cordelia.
                            They
                            know
                            each
                            other
                            half
                            as
                            well
                            as

they
should
have.
    And,
        says
    Bilbo,
            "I
like
    less
        than
            half
                of
                    you
half
    as
        well
            as
                you
                    deserve."

My
brother
(or
is
it
me?)
soon
requests
a
room
change
from
the

adults:
build
a
brick
wall
in between,
a
marker,
a
border.
The
command
is
made:
create
two
rooms—
separate
but
equal—
one
for
each
sibling,
ich
und
du,
with
two
doors,
two
desks,
two
closets,
two
twos.

Mother
complies
but
  only
    after
telling
a
  Kafkaesque
  story
(Kafka:
patron saint of negation):
  the man
  from
  the country
  comes
  before
  a
  wall,
she
says,
  a
  wall
  that
  is
  at
  the
  edge
  of
  the
  kingdom.
Next
to
the
door
is
a
gatekeeper.

"Can
I
get
out?"
asks
the man.
"Out?"
wonders
the
gatekeeper.
"You
mean
in?"
"No,"
responds
the
man.
"Out
of
the
kingdom."
The
gatekeeper
laughs:
"The
kingdom
starts
on
other side,
but
that
side
is
not for you,
at
least
not now.

You
must
earn
your
place
in
it."
"How?"
asks
the
man.

"By
always
staying
on
this
side,"
answers
the
gatekeeper.

In
a
2008
navy-blue
Toyota
that
burps
every time
I
brake,
I
make
my
way
to
narrow-minded

Matamoros
    ("mata moros"),
and
near
an OXXO
I
hear
a
gunshot
and
    poooof!
But
I
see
a bloody
corpse
covered
in
plastic.
It
has
been
there
a
couple
of hours,
I
am told.
    She
    is
    youngish
        and
    so
    are
    the onlookers
(except
me).

No
one
does
a thing
(including me):
the
ubiquity
of
death.
                    A
                                    couple
            nearby
kisses
            and
                            a
            boy
sucks
his
            lollipop.
"Uy,"
a
mustachio
policeman
says
to
me:
"Ni se acerque,
señor.
It
will
be
cleaned
up
shortly!
It's
much
worse

in
Reynosa.
Ask
people
to
tell
you
about
the
pool
of
tears
in
the Catedral."
      The
      policeman
      talks
      more,
      though
      not
      the kind
      of talk
      that
      fosters
      congruence.

My
mother
orders
the
brick
wall
built,
dividing
east
from
west:

my
room
for him,
my
brother's
room
not
for me—
no
longer
one
single,
boundless
room.

¡ALTO!
My
brother
and
I
grow up:
as
adults,
we
are
selfish,
venal,
even
mercenary:
suspicious
of
one
another.
Suspicion
becomes
wariness,
skepticism,

mistrust.
Paradise
is
now
made
of
halves:
two
doors,
two
desks,
two
twos.

Near
Ciudad Río Bravo,
on
2D,
an hour
and
a half
later,
the
Toyota
is
dead,
too.
I
am
desolate.
It
is
107 degrees.
Upset
and
afraid,
I

wave
at
a truck.
The
driver
says
he'll
rush
his
cousin
back
to me
in
15
minutes.
I'm
incredulous!
Yet,
miracle of
miracles,
Raúl,
a
29 year-old
mechanic
with
a workshop
on La Esperanza,
works
on
jumpstarting
my
engine,
but,
after
much sound and fury,
suggests
I

exchange
it
for
a
1998
VW:
"Újule, señor,
si no
usted 'stará
estancado
en
este valle de lágrimas
hasta
el día
del
Juicio Final."
I
comply
and
 go,
   goo,
     gooo . . .
He tells
me
to
visit
a
house
with
"as
many
bullet holes
as
a
slice
of
Swiss cheese.

But,
oye,
la gente
sigue
viviendo.
¿o no?"

¡SILENCIO!
Go,
goo
gooo:
fast,
faster,
fastest:
run
like
hell
and
don't
look
back.
Near Zapata,
adjacent
to
the
Falcon International Reservoir,
the ringtale,
javelina,
the rattlesnake,
and
the gila woodpecker,
as
well
as
the
Anna's hummingbird,

will
gather
at my side.
They
are
watching
over
me.

      ¡Corre, cabrón!
      Coorre,
      cooorre,
      coooorre,
      no
      seas pendejo:
      el
      mundo
      termina
      aquí.
      Este
      es
      el culo
      y no la cara.

      ¡Síguele, cabrón!
      Coorre,
      cooorre,
      coooorre,
      no
      seas puto:
      el
      mundo
      termina
      aquí.
      Esta
      es
      la cara

del
culo.
¡Qué onda, cabrón!
Coorre,
cooorre,
coooorre,
no
seas culero:
el
mundo
termina
aquí.
Es
caro
el
temor
y
es chulo
el
dinero.

Chinga
chingón,
chingando
chingaderas.
¡Chíngatelas!
Huevo,
huevón,
huevero,
huevadera.
¡Que hueva
quien
hueva!
Chíngate
los
huevos,

hijo
de
tu
madre.
I
sleep—
"have
I
been
asleep
all
this
long?"—
in
a
motel
in Ciudad Acuña,
near
Lake Amistad,
where
twisters
carry
the
sour
pain of
balaceados,
those
whose
bodies
become
bullet holders.
Each
family
I talk to
has
relatives

dispersed
across
hundreds
of thousands
of miles.
Doña Leticia
shows
an old photo:
Miguel Fulgencio Fuentes,
last seen
on
October
19,
2007,
at a gas station
in Piedras Negras.
Raimundo Rodríguez López,
her nephew,
will look for Amilia Díaz López
in Wichita Falls.
And Diego Henríquez
no
longer
knows
if Gabriela Durán
is his
girlfriend.
Her
phone number:
sorry,
the number
you
have
dialed,
(718) 567–2349,
has
been

disconnected.
El
número
que
usted
marcó,
(718) 567–2349,
no
está
en
servicio.
¿Servicio?
Ser
vicio.
Diego Henríquez
is
no
more.
Gabriela Durán
has
been
gone
for
years.
Ella
no
está
en
servicio.
Ella
no
está.
Ella?
No . . .

El
muro,
　　the
　　　　wall:
　　　　　　"Do
　　　　　　　　you
　　　　　　　　　　think
　　　　　　　　　　it
　　　　　　　　　　is
　　　　　　　　　　an
　　　　　　　　　　illusion?"
　　　　　　　　　　a
　　　　　　　　　　pastor
　　　　　　　　　　asks
　　　　　　　　　　me.
Reaching
　　heaven,
　　　　the
　　　　　　wall
　　　　　　　giveth,
　　　　　　　　　the
　　　　　　　　　wall
　　　　　　　　　taketh
　　　　　　　　　away.
　　　　　　　　　Whoever
　　　　　　　　　climbs
　　　　　　　　　higher,
　　　　　　　　　runs
　　　　　　　　　faster,
　　　　　　　　　and
　　　　　　　　　is a
　　　　　　　　　fool's
　　　　　　　　　fool,
　　　　　　　　　whoever
　　　　　　　　　shines
　　　　　　　　　a
　　　　　　　　　white
　　　　　　　　　smile—

                    happy
                          to
                               be
                                    on
                                         camera—
                                              is
                                              tonight's
                                              winner.

Mournful
restrain:
in Ciudad Juárez,
across
from
El Paso,
be
sure
to look
at
the
lovers—

                                              "the
                                              words
                                              'amor
                                              loco'
                                              are
                                              tattooed
                                              on
                                              all
                                              their
                                              foreheads"—,
and
make
yourself
at
home
with
cacti,

cholla,
ocotillo,
marigold.
Find
comfort
under
the
Foothill
Paloverde.
Chew
peyote.
The
antlions
will
build
a colony
in
your
liver.
Wasps
will
incubate
in
your
ears.
Crickets
and
grasshoppers
and
beetles
and
moths
and
flies
will
eat
your

carcass.
All
will
sing
their
national
anthem:
    diptera,
    hymenoptera,
    coleoptera,
    lepidoptera,
    neuroptera,
    and
    orthoptera
        of
        the
        planet,
        unionize.

My
mother
agreed
to
a
separation:
the
room
is
no
more:
one,
two—
another
brick
in the wall.
I
look

at
pictures
of
my
brother,
just
as
he
probably
looks
at
photos
of me.

At
the
    threshold
    of
        the
        kingdom,
            the
            question
                is
                uttered:
                    who
                    are YOU?

U
r
u
are
TÚ ...
Y
tú
eres
lumps,
various
and
unformed,

every
piece
playing,
at
every
second,
su
propio
juego.
And
el
jugo
del
juego
is
proof
that
—¡sorpresa!—
no
hay
diferencia
entre
us
y
ourselves
o
between
nosotros
and
los otros.

II. WHO WHOES THE WHO?

¡ATENCIÓN!
Pero nadie te oye . . .
America
is
home
to romantics.
All
are
busy
at
work:
incessant,
industrious,
back
and
forth,
coming and going.
Ziggurats
are built
by
deranged
architects
at astonishing
speed.
The skyline
changes
every second,
nothing
lasts
a day:

cities
rise
and fall.
　　　　The tyranny of the new.
　　　　New
　　　　is
　　　　young.
　　　　Young
　　　　is
　　　　original.
　　　　Original
　　　　is
　　　　novel.
　　　　Novel
　　　　is
　　　　fresh.
　　　　Fresh
　　　　is
　　　　different.
　　　　Different
　　　　is
　　　　desirable.

Each
wall
is
made
of
bricks,
cement,
beams,
plaster.
Yet
walls
alone,
disengaged,

don't
result
in
anything—
but
in
walls
alone,
disengaged
and
nothing . . .

Excess:
more is more.
   The future
   is
   a work
   in
   progress.
It
isn't
now
but
across the line:
mañana,
a promise
delayed.

   ¡Muro de mierda!
The
ghost
of
my brother
a cuestas,
I've
walked

most
of it,
along
zigzagging miles,
through the coagulum
of the gangrened river,
fetid,
ghoulish,
its perimeter
renouncing life.
Other
walls
are
sheer
preparation:
this,
THIS
is the wall
to end all walls.
No
other
imaginary
line
in the world
is crossed
more frequently;
no other line
in the planet
smells as fetid.

       Sí, patrón:
       tis' the end of my South,
       and tis'
       the end of your North.

Just move:
go, go go . . .

in motion,
though the motions:
No espeak inglés?
Just pretend,
amigo.
Over there
not everyone
speaks
the language
either.
¡Gracias, gringuito!
I love you more than
you'll ever know.

Puta madre:
El Camino del Diablo,
the road
where the Devil tallies.
See them:
thousands of crucifixes
irrigate the land.
Souls,
yours,
mine,
lying underneath—
a final pose,
awaiting
resurrection,
a chorus of
laments,
murmurs,
laughter.
These
are
the souls
of
brave

women and men,
who struggled here.
They
have
consecrated
this
unfertile
ground
above and beyond
our
poor
to add or detract.
        Death
is unfinished work,
and
it is left to US,
        witnesses
                        to their dismay,
to
do
the unfinished work
they
so
nobly advanced:
to bring food to our tables,
to make us believe
we are free,
to allow us the dream
of being
a
nation.

A nation
without
a
backbone?

No,
eradicate
their
memory:
cut
them out.
Use them,
abuse them,
ignore
their
plight.
Build
a wall—
higher,
stronger,
mightier . . .
Don't U see it yet?
It isn't steep enough,
tough enough,
firm enough.
It
isn't
bloody
enough.
For
we have decided
to stick
to hate.
Love is too great
a burden
to bear.
Far
stronger
than
love
is hate.

All together now:
WE WILL BUILD A HUGE WALL.
A BEAUTIFUL WALL.
And YOU,
you,
u,
will pay for it,
a wall
from sea to shining sea
(though 1,959 miles
of mainland,
plus 18 more maritime miles
in the Pacific,
and 12 in the Gulf)
a wall
to
leave out
BAD HOMBRES.

El Presidente:
the Founding Fathers
are
rolling in their graves.
The Chinese Emperor
Shih Huang Ti
(also known as Qin Shi Huang),
who
in
221 B.C.E.
built
the original Great Wall of China,
hated
his mother.
Such
was
his
abhorrence

that
he
decided
to
forever
erase her
from
memory.
But
how
does
one
expurgate
memory?
By
destroying
its
foundations.
                    Thus,
                            Shih Huang Ti
            ordered
the burning
            of
all books
                    in
                            the kingdom.
History
starts
here,
history
starts
now.

Shih Huang Ti
erected
the Great Wall
to

defend
the kingdom
from its enemies.
But
the wall
brought
along
a
collateral
problem:
isolating
China
from
its neighbors.

Later on,
the length
of
the
Great Wall
during
the Ming Dynasty
was
5,500.3 miles,
from Hushan
in
Liaoning
to
Jiayuguan Pass
in
Gansu:
bigger,
faster,
smarter,
heftier,
richer.

Be a tourist,
take a tour:
climb
its
steep
staircases
and
dwindling
vertebrae:
the wall
is a tourist
attraction.
Money,
happiness,
selfies.
Yet
it
remains
a
carcass,
the
skeleton
of
false
aspirations.

Sherwood Anderson,
creator of
Winesburg, where
clocks
never hurry,
answers:
yes,
true,
"Women
and men
lead their lives

behind a wall
of misunderstanding,
a wall they themselves built,
and
most
women and men
die
in silence
and
unnoticed behind that wall."
He
is
right
on
the mark.

       "But
       once in a while
       someone,
       cut off
       from
       the rest
       by the peculiarities of nature,
       becomes absorbed
in doing
something
that is personal,
useful
and beautiful.
       Word of such activities
       is
       carried
       over the wall.
That someone
might
be green,
blue,

yellow,
and brown."
That
someone
is
a hero.

Isaac's father
is
taking him
to
the
top.
The
fence
is
called
Moriah.
Call
it
terram visionis.
Or
Marwah,
which
is
in Mecca.
Or
call
it
Reja de Satanás,
where
a
sign
reads:
"Más
sabe
el

diablo
por
viejo
que
por
diablo.
How
easy
is
it
to
judge
wrongly
after
what
good
comes
from
judging
rightly?"
"Where are we going?"
the boy asks.
"The Lord
has
announced
to me
this road,"
the father
responds.
"He wants
our
deliverance.
We shall offer Him
a sacrifice.
A lamb will satisfy Him."
Isaac,
7 years-old,

smiles.
Father and son
climb
at night.
The desert
is
never
still:
if you're quiet,
you
might
hear the wind;
if you're alert,
you
might
see
the moon's
dress
in
all
its
splendor.
"Once we're at the top,
I'll hold you tight,
me oyes?"
orders the father.
"Where is the sacrificial lamb?"
"The Lord giveth
and
the Lord taketh away.
The lamb waits for us at the top."
No guards.
The father pulls up his son Isaac.
Once at the top,
the father
takes
a screwdriver

out
of his leather jacket.
It
will
help
loosen
the fence.
The moon
glitters,
its
reflection
multiplied
on
the apathetic steel.
The father's left hand
chokes
the son—
"no
puedo
respirar, apá!"—,
as
the right
hand
descends,
turning
the
fatal
screwdriver
into
a
rigorous
weapon.

STOP!
A sniper.
Isaac's father
falls,

lifeless
to the ground.
The boy
shrieks.
The
border patrol
asks
the boy
to climb
down:
      DOWN.
"Where is the sacrificial lamb?"
inquires Isaac.
No,
the questions are:
who is the Angel of Death?
And
where is the Angel of Life?
Who saved Isaac?
and
from what?
Or better,
did anyone
remember
to
save
the child?
Blood
spills
on
the ground,
a stream
from
the father's chest
onto
the cold cement.
Isaac

places
his
fingers
in it:
hot,
cold.

        I *am* brown,
        the color of bronze,
coffee,
        mud,
vigor.
        Look at me:
I am
the bricklayer,
the organ grinder,
the glass blower,
the milkman.
De este lado
también
tenemos
sueños.
It is
by accident
that
we were born on this side
and
not in the other.
        The Zetas
            are
                in
                recruitment
                mode.
                Beware
                of
                the Halcones:
                they

spy
on
you.
Either
you
are
in
or
you
are
dead.
Careful
what you wish,
cuate:
tomorrow
you
might
find
yourself
on
the other
side.

Sí, sí, canijo,
pero, nanitas,
the Wall
won't stop
the pounding.
Ya verás . . .
"If they go low,
we go high;
If they go high,
we go low."

And it won't
stop
the music,

the symphony
of names:
from Chihuahua,
Abelardo Bustos,
Cristina Dolores Enríquez,
Fabián González Hernández Ibáñez;
from Nogales,
Juanita Karlín,
Leticia Martínez Noguera,
Ofelia and Pedro Quintana Ruíz;
from Sonora,
Sandra Torres,
Ulises Vladimiro Walter Xalis Yáñez,
Zoila Yunque Xavier Whitman;
from Durango,
Data Denata,
Dota Darota Debota,
Dabrila Donzález Donzález Donzález;
de Tijuana,
Túmulo Teimbla
Torcuato Tímpano Tremebundo
Tercio Trapecio Trémulo Tricornio . . .

¡Fíjate!
It ain't bricks
but stories—
it's what the Wall
is made of:
cuentos,
the stories
flying,
free-wheeling,
flowing,
floooooooooowin',
stories about people,
inside people,
stories

across neighborhoods,
and pueblos,
desiertos,
stories told by birds,
cobras,
cacti,
daffodils,
rocks and
dusty
roads,
loose stories,
speedy,
unstructured,
stories
uninhibited,
boundless—
the Devil's
stories.

Who?
Thousands
of
miles
from
sea
to
shrinking
sea.
Think:
Washington, D.C.,
is
only 68.34 square miles.
Who excludes
who?
Who
whoes
the who?

History
will
judge us
not by how powerful
we are
but by the depth
and
endurance
of
our compassion.

I
who
the WHO.
You
who
the YOU.
Enough
with
south is SOUTH
and
north is NORTH
and
never
the two
shall meet.
North
goes
south
and
south
goes
north.
¡ÁNDALE!

III. THE OPPOSITE OF INDIFFERENCE

                          Why
            do
            I feel compelled
                          to recline
                                        in
                          front
                                        of
                                                    walls?

Near
Las Palomas,
eyes
weary,
tank
almost
empty,
my
VW
under
a
blanket
of
dust,
driving
in circles,
trapped
by
the
ghosts
inside
my mind,

I
pray
to
the Almighty
as
I
spot
copters
circling
the sky.
Dogs bark.
One,
two
gunshots.
A
scream,
"These
aren't
humans;
they are roaches."
But nothing,
no one,
ceases
to
move:
these
are
the
natural
sounds
of
nature.
          This
          is
          Chihuahua,
          where

Ambrose Bierce
disappeared,
the
         wound—
                  la herida abierta—
         where
the First
and Third
Worlds
poke
fun
at
their
misery.
An
injury
is
a
reminder
of
trauma.
And
I
cry
as
I
have cried before
other
walls
tears of antiquity
while
others
have
wailed
with
me.

                    The
                        wall
                            was
                        on the western
                    side of the temple.
It
is
the sole remnant
after
repeated destruction,
the
last
standing
structure,
a
testament
to
incessant wars
inspired
by a vengeful god:
105 feet,
exposed,
holy,
built in
19 B.C.E.
by Herod the Great:
the western
structure
in David's
Temple.

                                        Every Tisha be-Av
                                        all
                                        of
                                        us,
                                        believers
                                        and
                                        cynics,

lament
the fracturing
of rememberance,
our dispersion
through
the world:
not
a
grand
wall
but
a
reminder—
and
remainder—
of
our
disembodied
selves:
everywhere
and nowhere—
with
a center
that
can't deliver
us
from our affliction
yet . . .

            Lacking
            any
        other
paper,
            I
        write,
on
        the

                back
of a business
                card
a
message
                            to
                                    the Almighty:
"make
Yourself
apparent
—NOW—
by
destroying
this
and
other walls."
I add:
"Stop
fostering
hatred.
Be
a
unifier,
not
a
divider."
I
insert
my
message
in
a crevice.
Ah,
I tell myself:
the
sanitation
department

will
clear it
and all others
inserted
today
by dawn
tomorrow.
That's
how
fast
the
Almighty
needs
to read.

A
wall
to
communicate
with
heaven
and
not
a telephone?
Bah,
all these
are
a
fool's
scribbles
signifying nothing.

BAH:
life matters!
But not all lives
matter in the same way.
Blacks

and
whites
and
yellows
and greens:
we
are all
many
and
our affliction
is our
circumstance:
peace is a mirage;
the plight
of humanity
is
through opposition.
"No
Mexicans
allowed!"
Rest
is
only
possible
in
death.

This
wall
is
old
but
the nation
that surrounds it
is young.
Tourists
(shooting
photos

again—
such conceit,
such narcissism)
wander
as
they
wonder,
near
Coptic
priests,
devout
nuns,
and a Japanese
marathoner.
This
is Muslim land
and Jewish
and Christian.
All
afterlives
converge
in
this
parched
ground.
Look,
souls
are
roaming
in
Mamilla Pool,
attaching
themselves
to
invisible
obelisks,
twirling
with

Emir Aidughdi Kubaki.
In
Mount Zion,
souls
are
gamboling:
Samuel Gobat,
Conrad Shick,
Michael Solomon Alexander,
William Irvine,
George Francis Graham Brown,
Max Sandreczky,
and
Lewis Yelland Andrews.
Souls
are
roving
in
Mount Olives,
where
the Silwan necropolis
is.
This
is
also
where Sukkot
is celebrated,
where all
Jews
mourn,
and
where
the
resurrection of
the dead
shall
start,

according
to
the
Book of Zechariah,
as Yaweh,
standing
in
Mount Olives,
will
witness
the mountain
splitting in two,
one half
shifting north
and one
half shifting south.
Mount Olives
is
layered
with generations
grieving
destruction,
the wall
their
sole
spokes-channel:
death
is
with us
though
there
is
no
wall
between
the living and
the dead—

only a thin,
discreet
veil.

Following
the war
of 1967,
soldiers
embraced
it
under
their
control.
An
infinite
number
of wishes
written
on paper
—like
mine—
are
inserted in
its fissures:
messages
sent
directly
to
heaven.

But
the wall
cries
because
women
and men
aren't heard
equally

by the divine.
It
howls
when
Yaweh and
Allah
are
antonyms.

Not
far
away,
Mahmood
and Aviva
and
Noor
and Avital
and
Sholem
exchange
shekels
for bread
and sweat,
with
a cursory
Salaam Aleikum
to keep
the sundown
as
placeholder
until
tomorrow.
Mahmood
and
Noor
display
their documents
on the

checkpoint
on
their way
home.

Home:
the sounds
are
different
in Arabic
and Hebrew.
Sounds
are bullets.

Not
far
away,
another wall,
tearful,
in
segregated
Jerusalem
is
the
Separation Wall,
וומת ההפרדה
and
العنصري الفصل جدار,
440 miles
splinting
Jews
and
Arabs,
partly
on
the "Green Line"
of the Jordanian-Israeli

Armistice
of 1949,
an apartheid
contour
of
stones
and
tanks.

Does
Nogales
dream
of
Jerusalem?
Does
Jerusalem
envy
Beijing?
Does
Beijing
emulate
Warsaw?
And
does
Warsaw
dream
of Jerusalem?
ACHTUNG!
Christa
Brandes
is
a
loudmouth.
She
privately
nurtures
a

scene
of immolation.
Not
far
from
Checkpoint Charlie,
Friday,
4pm,
as passers-by
look
in
astonishment,
she
will
pour
a liter
of
gasoline
on
the wall,
then
another
on
herself.
She
will
chant
—in
French—
"L'Internationale,"
singing
while
laughing,
laughing
while
shrieking,

"C'est la lutte finale
groupons-nous, et demain
L'Internationale
sera le genre humain."

Absolute
compliance:
no
one
is
allowed!
Dissent
is
strictly
forbidden!
The
Oder-Niesse line
divides
the
city
in
four
zones,
one
per
reigning
power:
United States,
France,
England,
and Josef Stalin.

Boundaries
are
needed:
the

wall
—all 11.81 miles—
divides
families,
neighbors,
friends.
The eye
of
STASI
records
every
move.

After
Nogales,
I
drive
off-route
to
Puerto Peñasco,
eat
tostadas de pollo
with
queso blanco,
frijoles negros,
and
una agua de tamarindo.
These
are
the
tastes of
my
childhood.
I
could
have been born
in Israel,

in South Africa,
in West Germany,
in New York,
but
I was born
in
Mexico City,
into
a
civilization
that
turns
resignation
into
grit.

Or
better:
I
was
born
into
Spanish,
and,
from it,
pushed
into
other languages.
Traversing
the border
is
for
me about reading
ads:
Duerma cómodo,
duerma con sábanas
La Hermosa;

Drink Coke;
DREAMers,
bienvenidos a su propia casa;
Wonder Bread,
the bread
that makes
you wonder;
Condones El Caballito,
para cuando menos lo piensas.
Dale, dale, dale,
no pierdas el tino
porque
si lo pierdes
pierdes el camino.

CABOOM!
An explosion
is
heard
from afar.
I
see
fire
on
the horizon
and
I think
of
the
Sbarro
pizzeria
that
still
displays
scars
of tragedy:
shrapnel
near

a bathroom door,
several
tables
always
uneven
on a floor
made volcanic
by
the
explosion
in
August 2001:
15 people killed,
including
7 children
and
a pregnant woman,
plus 130 wounded.
Each
one
is
unique,
each
one
is
the
whole
of
humanity.

Is
love
in
one
country
hate
in
another?

Poor Mexico,
so
far
from
God
and
so
close
to the United States.
And
poor
United States,
so
caught
up in false cheerfulness
and
so
close to
its own despondency.
I
think
of
June 2014
when,
after
the abduction
of three
Israeli
teenagers,
Israel
launched
Operation Brother's Keeper
in Gaza
against
Hamas:
11 Palestinians
were

killed
and
51 were
wounded
in 369 Israeli incursions
plus
between 350 and 600 Palestinians
were arrested.
Each
one
is
unique,
each
one
is
the
whole
of
humanity.

A valley
of
tears.
Walls,
enclosures,
barriers:
like Janus,
hypocritical,
duplicitous,
two-sided.
Joy
on one
side,
fear
in
the other.

As of July 2011:
272 miles
were finished,
with 36 miles under construction,
and 132 miles planned.
After
July 2011:
a trillion miles
minus 272 unfinished,
with 798,231,639
dreams under destruction,
and zero
hope
scheduled.

Freedom
is
one:
total,
unflinching,
and
undividable.
It
cannot
be
inhibited,
subdued,
and
withdrawn.
Freedom
is
one
and
cannot
be
split
in
two.

                    It
          cannot
          be
          given
          to one
                    and
                         taken
                                   away
                                        from
                                                  another.

Oh,
East is East
and
West is West
and
never
the two
shall meet,
in
spite
of
the
prophet's
message:
"The opposite of love is not hate
but indifference.
The opposite of art is not ugliness
but indifference.
The opposite of faith is not heresy but indifference.
And the opposite of life is not death
but indifference."

Jews
know how cold
the walls
of crematoria are.
They

know how firm
ghetto walls
feel.
The wall
of
the Warsaw
ghetto
(where
my
father's
mother
was
born)
has
been
      chipped
      away.

            Fist-size
            holes
            are
            blocked
            with
            dirty,
            wet
            cloth.

YOU
are
able
to
talk
across it,
send
written
messages
(though
not
on

business
cards),
get
a
package
of cigarettes,
a bottle
of milk,
pass
a
few
coins.

Isn't
information
like
oxygen?
It seeps
across,
unimpeded,
fostering
dreams
of
democracy.

Thirsty,
I
park
the
exhausted
VW
on
an empty
sidewalk,
eat
tacos de pescado
and

look
for
rest
in
a Holiday Inn
on
a dull
road:
nadie,
nada,
nunca.

Holiday Inn:
our
best
rate
is
waiting for you!
Members
now
get
better
savings,
every
bed
is
a king's
bed
and
every
table
is
a kid's
table.
Relax:
welcome
to

far
more
than
the expected.
Drink
the
milk
of
PARADISE
and
have
the
journey
of
your
life.
These
walls
are
yours.

IV. MY SWEET ENEMY

                                        Pitiful
                                        erection—
                                        slayer
                                        of desire
                                        and
                                        carbuncle
                                        of
                                        regrets.

             Mark Twain
                     said
                                    that
                history
doesn't repeat itself
                     but
it does rhyme.
I
          give
up
                     the VW:
                     an aleph,
                     lejos del mundanal ruido.
It
is
time
to
walk
the
walk.

In
Tijuana,
I
sit
at
a
bar
called
La Inconsciencia,
sipping
Coronas.
Acid
rain
is
falling
outside.
The
owner
shows
me
a map
of Mexico
prior
to
1835:
it
includes
Alta California,
New Mexico,
and
the "disputed
territory."
"Whose
Manifest Destiny?"
the
owner asks.
"We're

NOT
taking
anything
away
that
wasn't
ours
in
the first
place."
He
adds:
"They
call
it
Southwest.
Southwest
of
what?
Southwest
de
mierda."
I
titter.
He
opens
another
chela
for me.
        "You
        professor,
        verdá?

                Sure
                as
                hell
                you're NOT
                from

around
these
lands.
       Have
       you
       told
       them
       about
       Aztlán?"

He
smiles:
       "They
       listen
       to
       you
       because
       of
       the
       color
       of
       your skin:
       blanquito."

              Angst,
              miedo,
              apprehension.

                            "Órale,
                            tell
                            the Gringos
                            about
                            the Real Magic
                            Kingdom,
                            the Kingdom of
                            Aztlán.

              It's
              the

Xanadu
of
the Aztecs.
You
know
where
Aztlán was,
o qué,
Profe?
Like
Tamoanchan,
Cibola,
Tollan,
and
Chicomoztoc,
Aztlán
is
everywhere
and
nowhere—
a place
of heroes
and heroines
(and heroin addicts).
Alfredo Chavero
believed
it
was
on
the
Pacific Coast,
maybe
in
Nayarit.
Others
think
Aztlán
is

in
Jalisco,
Michoacán,
or
Guanajuato.
Take
your
pick,
profe,
as
long
as
you find it,
since
Aztlán,
de veras,
is
the
loin,
el
paraíso.
And
a loin
cannot
be
divided."

He pauses.
The
music—
"Sing the Real,"
followed
by
"Die Cowboy Die,"
followed
by
"Queztanimales"—

is
suddenly
loud:
Lucha Villa,
José Alfredo Jiménez,
Juan Gabriel.
The owner
says:
"I'm gonna show
you Aztlán.
Come with me!"
I
follow
him
behind
a curtain
into
another room,
down
a
staircase,
across
a
refrigerated
chamber,
into
a
dark
area
after
which
we
enter
a shrine.
A
sign
on

the
wall
reads,
in English:
"Dante's Circle #6:
The Denial of Immortality!"
At
a
distance,
I
listen
to
women
half-heartedly
whistling
"La Cucaracha."

Flowers,
candle sticks,
fruit,
framed images
of La Virgen,
Frida,
María Sabina,
El Santo,
Reies López Tijerina,
Dolores Huerta,
and
Cesar Chavez,
as well as
Benito Juárez,
Lincoln,
and
Obama:
offerings
in
an altar.

I
see
a
doll
of
Trump
with
black
marks all over.
The
incense
makes
me
imagine
Jerusalem.
I
have
a
vision
in
a
dream.
Am
I
in
a
junkyard?
      "Aztlán,
      carajo!"
      the
      owner
      says
      while
      pouring
      tequila
      on
      the altar:

"Sálvanos,
pecadores.
Devuélvenos
lo
perdido,
lo
nuestro.
Complétanos
para
que seamos
quienes
debemos
ser."

The
vision
inside
the
dream:
a sacred river,
measureless caverns
a sunless sea
and
a
pleasure-dome
with walls and towers
and gardens
bright
with sinuous rills.
The shadow of the dome of pleasure
floats midway on the waves
as
I close my eyes
to
see a Nahuatl princess
who will revive me from my stupor.
"Beware!

Beware!"
she screams
and
pours
on me a glass of milk
I
stole
from the Holiday Inn.

I
don't
leave
La Inconsciencia
until
late,
after
the owner
agrees
to
call
a
taxi
for
me.
Yes,
a
junkyard
of
yearnings,
I
tell
myself.

                    I
                    have
                    seen
                    countless
                    sunsets,

I
have
drank
from
the
fountain
of
sorrow.
I
want
to
go
home.

But
home
is
gone:
you
are neither
from
here
nor
from
there.
The
never-ending
room
is
no
more.
Only the wall survives:
my
brother
and
I,
apart,

distant,
unknown
to
one
another.
The
wall
is
us.
The
wall
between
yesterday
and
tomorrow.
Mañana,
señores.
Mañana
es
siempre
mejor.
Cheap
talk—
it
comes
easy.

Tomorrow
and tomorrow
and tomorrow
creeps
in
this pretty pace.
And
all our
yesterdays
have
guided

a
troupe
of
idiots
on
their
way
to
filthy
deaths.

Fast
faaster
faaastest . . .
Vámonos, cuates.
Aquí
nadie nos quiere.
Back
and
forth,
I touch its texture:
the wall
hardens my
fingertips.
In
Douglas,
Arizona,
I
find
Isabella
La Reyna,
whose
siblings
stayed in Guatemala.
In El Paso,
un viejo
me dice
que Dios es feliz

and
that we are also,
in spite of spite.
    "¡Felicidad a como dé lugar!"
He
tells
me
freedom
isn't an option
but
an obligation.
     "We
        have
           to be
       libres
     even when we don't like it."
In Algodones Dunes,
I
bottle
sand.
It
is sacred,
I tell myself,
like
the
sand of Jerusalem,
the
sand
in
the
Holy Land.
In
Imperial Valley,
Mexicali,
teenagers
make
bonfires
to

warm
themselves up
with
American
and
Mexican
flags.
And
I
spend
the night
drinking
ayahuasca
with
a whore
whose
wisdom
holds
ancestral
secrets.

Finally,
after
six
days
(y
sus
noches),
alone,
unencumbered,
traversing
the
land,
I
come
to
the
end,

where
the
gatekeeper
is
waiting
for me.
His—I see now—is my mother's face.
"Can
I
get
out?"
I
ask.
"Out?"
wonders
the
gatekeeper.
"Out
of
the
kingdom,"
I
say.
The
gatekeeper,
bashful,
giggles:
"The
kingdom
is
you."
He
hands me
a hammer.
"Do
you
think
the time

has
come?
Go ahead,
bring
the
wall
down.
It
was
you
who
asked
for it,
not your brother.
You
are
the ruler
of
the kingdom:
ADELANTE.
Now
you
can destroy it
because
everything
that
is
made
contains
within
itself
a desire
for
its unmaking.

I see masks:
Isaac's father,
the corpse

abandoned in
the
Sonora Desert.
A Minute-Man.
A lavandera.
A plumber.
I see
the deprecating banker,
arrogant plumber,
and tedious teacher,
the abusive taxi driver,
the facetious actor,
and
the hopeful real-estate agent.
The
shrewd coyote,
the procrastinating senator,
the rasping drug dealer,
and the gentle girl
are
looking for
work
in a maquiladora.
The journalist
and
the translator
and the activist
are
self-referentially
lending
their
voice
to
others.
Plus,
I see
the anonymous
face

of the masses
that
thrive
in
indifference.
All
are
lumps.
All
are
my enemy,
my sweet enemy,
like
Don Quixote's
Dulcinea,
which,
—wonder
of
wonders—
is
me . . .

I
hammer.
I hammer . . .
The wall
comes
down
but
not its specter,
which
contains
in
itself
all
other
walls.
On

the
ground,
I stumble
upon
the
message
I
wrote
to
the Almighty:
"make
Yourself
apparent
—NOW—
by
destroying
this
and
other walls."
Trembling,
I
hear
laughter.
I
continue:
"If I exist at all,
if I am not one of Your repetitions
and
errata,
I exist as the author of *The Wall*.
In order to conclude this poem,
which may serve to justify me,
to justify You,
I need a miracle,
You,
to whom
belong the centuries
and all time.

Make
that
miracle
our
reconciliation."

The
laughter
becomes
louder.
A
voice
announces:
"Your
wish
has
been
granted."
A
sudden
peace
in
me
explodes,
an
exhilarating
feeling,
the
conviction
that
I
have
not
traversed
the
edges
of
the kingdom

in
vain.

Suddenly,
in
attempting
to
touch
the shadow,
the
altar
in
La Inconsciencia
takes
over
my
surroundings:
I
have
surrendered
my
will,
I
am
an
offering.

Sure
as
hell
you're NOT
from
around
these
lands.
In
San Diego,
where

Gaspar de Portolá
established
a
presidio
overseeing
San Diego Bay,
on
the land
of
the Kumeyaay,
who
revolted
(so the Spaniards
built
a stockade),
I sense
the
white teeth
of
the
American Smile
on
me,
arguing
that
        "Hey, hey,
        all is
                forgotten
                and
        life
        is
        cool!"
It isn't, though.

                    Vicious,
                    mystifying,
                    the embolism
                    of

countless
miles
is
behind
me
and
also
in
my
guts.

Mightier
than
ever,
      I long
      for
          home.
But
this
is
home,
too.

El
final,
the
end.
Is
it
better
to
burn out
than
to
fade away?
El
principio

del
final
es
otro
principio.

The
landscape
scans
my
imagination.
The
end
is
the beginning
and
the
beginning
is
the end.
There
is
no end
to
the
journey.
There
is
no
end
to the end.
Death
is
always
waiting.
Death
is
the

only
path.
Death
is
on
the
other
side
of the
precipice.

Death
is
total
freedom.
Death
is
the
end
of
freedom.
I
realize
now
that
the
room,
the
wall,
the
altar,
and
I
        are
           all
               made
                  of . . .